Adventures
of Mr. Bill

Adventures of Mr. Bill

Humorous tales from the life of a school bus driver

Written by Bill Parrish
Illustrated by Dick Evans

YELLOW BUS PUBLISHING
Traverse City, Mich.

Yellow Bus Publishing
Traverse City, Mich.

Parrish, Bill.
  Adventures of Mr. Bill: humorous tales from the life of a school bus driver / written by Bill Parrish ; illustrated by Dick Evans. — Traverse City, Mich. : Yellow Bus Publishing, c2008.

    p. : ill. ; cm.

    ISBN: 978-0-9799145-0-8

    1. School children—Transportation—Humor. 2. Bus driving—Humor. 3. School buses—Humor.   I. Evans, Dick. II. Title. III. Title: Adventures of Mister Bill.

LB2864 .P37 2008   2007938441
371.8/72—dc22   0712

Printed in the United States of America
10 9 8 7 6 5 4 3 2 1

Book design by To The Point Solutions
www.tothepointsolutions.com

www.yellowbuspublishing.com

To my grandson, Joshua.
And to his mother, teachers, aides, bus drivers, and the nurses
who have nurtured and loved him so that, despite his physical
and mental handicaps, he has reached maturity with a sunny outlook
that enriches the lives of everyone he touches.

CONTENTS

SEVENTH THROUGH TWELFTH GRADE
ADOLESCENCE TO RELATIONSHIPS

INTRODUCTION

The first and last school-affiliated person most students encounter during the week is the school bus driver. In addition to providing transportation, bus drivers help students with their homework, listen to their woes, and share in their triumphs. By the end of each school year we are a family, of sorts. And just like in any family, humor abounds.

The names and places have been changed to protect the guilty. The illustrations do not resemble the actual people involved in each incident—well, *maybe* a little!

The memoirs for this book were compiled from my actual experiences and from a few fellow school bus drivers. If you enjoy the book, please tell your friends about Mr. Bill, the school bus driver. If you have any objections to the book, tell them Steve wrote it.

Kindergarten through Sixth Grade

INNOCENCE TO ATTITUDE

"How OLD is he?!"

FIRST BUS RIDE

It is the beginning of the school year. I am accompanying another bus driver to visit a class of kindergartners prior to taking them on their first bus ride. As I explain the boarding and unloading procedures to the excited children, one bright lad keeps raising his hand and asking questions.

We finally have the class on the bus. The boy immediately raises his hand and asks where the seat belt is. I explain that the seats on the school bus are especially designed for their protection so kids don't need seat belts—*but* they must stay seated at all times.

After digesting this information, the lad raises his hand. "Why is the driver wearing a seat belt?" he asks.

I explain that the driver keeps falling out of his seat so I have to put a belt on him to keep him in his chair.

The boy is quiet for a few minutes and then raises his hand again. "How *old* is he?"

"Ninety-two," I quickly respond.

Although the curious kindergartner finally remains silent, my thirty-year-old partner leans over and whispers to me, "I can hear the dispatcher getting a phone call from some anxious mother about a ninety-two-year-old bus driver who keeps falling out of his seat!"

KINDERGARTEN MOM

The start of a school year is always exciting, especially for the kindergartners and new students on the route. Everyone is euphoric.

As the bus approaches a stop, I see a mother with a camera in one hand and holding onto her daughter's hand with the other. The kindergartner is wearing a pretty new dress and has ribbons in her hair. When the bus stops she flashes a big smile of delight.

As I open the door, I greet the girl with a big, "Good morning! Welcome to your first bus ride!"

When she fails to board the bus, I realize the mother is caught up in the emotions of the event. Large tears streaming down her face. The little girl starts to comfort her mother. "It's okay, Mom," she says. "I'll be okay." The woman bursts into sobs.

As I wait, with red lights flashing and motorists lining up behind the bus, the girl tries to convince her mother everything is going to be all right. The woman's sobs grow louder. She finally manages to wave her arm toward me and says, "Just go on. I will drive her to school today. We can try it again tomorrow."

"Is your name Stacey?"

STOWAWAY

It is a beautiful spring afternoon. As I am driving my elementary route home, the dispatcher calls all bus drivers and asks us to look for a missing kindergartner named Stacey. None of the students on my route have that name, but after the next stop, I pull the bus over to the side of the road and get out of my seat to check the bus.

I am about halfway through the bus when I notice a little girl who I do not recognize sitting with one of my regular kindergarten students.

"Is your name Stacey?"

With a big smile, she replies, "Yes."

"Where are you going today on Mr. Bill's bus?" I ask.

"Home, with my friend Laura."

"Did you tell the school office?"

"No."

"Did you tell your teacher?"

"No."

"Do you normally ride a bus home?" I continue.

"No, my mom always picks me up."

"Did you ask your mother to go home with Laura?"

"No."

"Well, maybe I better call and tell everybody at school where you are," I say.

"Okay," she nonchalantly replies.

As I pick up the mike to call the bus dispatcher, I imagine the principal, teachers, secretary, and her mother freaking out while they search the entire school. The dispatcher immediately contacts the school and reports back to me that everybody is excited to get the news she has been found. "Her mother will meet you in the church parking lot at the end of your route," says the dispatcher.

"That is a big Ten-Four," I reply.

THE LITTLE TURTLE

One cold and icy morning I stop the bus on a slick rural road to pick up a third grader and her kindergartner sister. The older girl quickly climbs aboard the bus, but her much shorter sibling is a number of steps behind. The younger girl has obviously been dressed to ward off the elements by a caring parent. She can barely move in her overstuffed pink snowsuit, boots, mittens, scarf, and a stocking cap with the snowsuit hood pulled down over it. On her back is a large, bulging backpack.

The first bus step is almost chest high on her. As she swings her right foot up to the step, her left foot slips underneath her and she tumbles backward, landing on her backpack. With arms and legs flailing unsuccessfully in an attempt to turn herself over, she looks like a pink turtle on its back.

I quickly step off the bus and scoop her up, snowsuit, backpack, and all. To my relief she is giggling and has a smile on her face as I set her on the bus.

"Let me tell you about the boys."

ADVICE FROM AN EIGHT-YEAR-OLD

Before school bus drivers are assigned their own routes, they must be trained. Part of the training includes riding along with an experienced driver to observe routes, kids, discipline, driving situations, etc.

During my training, as a group of elementary students board the bus, an inquisitive young lady looks at me and says, "*Who* are *you?*"

I explain that I am in training to be a school bus driver and I am learning about kids.

"*Well*," she says, as she puts her hands on her hips, "let *me* tell you about the *boys* . . ."

MMFMF

As a first grader kisses his mom good-bye prior to boarding the bus, I watch her hand him a pack of gum. I think nothing of it . . . until later.

Once we are at school and the children get off the bus, I tell each of them to have a good day. Some nod their heads, others actually reply. When I give my standard farewell to this boy, I notice he has chipmunk cheeks and responds with, "*Mmfmf.*"

Before I leave the school parking lot, I always check the bus for lost lunches, forgotten books, etc. As I am picking up debris I find an empty gum pack and five wrappers on the floor.

He will make the teacher's day, I think to myself.

NEW STUDENT

As the elementary kids board the bus for the afternoon ride home, a handsome fifth grader hands me his new-student bus pass. I welcome him aboard and tell him to sit anywhere he likes. As he looks for a spot, I pick up the mike and introduce him to the other riders.

No sooner has he taken a seat in the middle of the bus when six girls gather around him. An argument ensues as to who will sit *next* to him, *behind* him, and *across* from him.

Throughout the route, I check the mirror and see him amongst six giggly girls who are talking simultaneously.

It is finally his stop. The red overhead lights are flashing, the door is open, and cars are lining up. Still, no one exits. I look in the mirror to see him surrounded by the girls. I grab the mike and announce, "Girls, we are holding up traffic. Please, let him off the bus."

As he departs, I ask, "So, how was your first day?"

His answer is a big grin.

SNOW WHITE AND HIS DWARFS

I have just pulled into the elementary school parking lot, with twenty-five passengers aboard, when I hear something roll out from underneath my seat and hit my left foot. A second later, I hear *Whoosh*! When I look down, I see a dry-chemical fire extinguisher discharging between my foot and the brake pedal.

With the heat and defrost blowers on full blast, the bus quickly fills with white powder. Visibility is deteriorating fast. I immediately stop the bus, shut off the extinguisher, and evacuate the students. As we gather outside the bus, it is apparent everyone is covered in white.

Even though I am six feet, two inches tall, I feel like Snow White and his twenty-five dwarfs.

"We're back at SCHOOL?!"

SURPRISE AND SHOCK

It is the afternoon ride home. I have only made it to the third stop, which is not far from the elementary school, when I receive a call from dispatch informing me that one of the students on board was supposed to have stayed at the school's latchkey program. I double back to school with a bus full of kids with voices at playground level, i.e., loud!

As I drive into the parking lot, a young lady shrieks, "We are back at SCHOOL!"

The silence is immediate. I look into the student mirror and see a bunch of students with stark terror on their faces. Seizing the moment, I grab the mike and announce, "You all were so noisy, I have brought you back to school." After a second's pause, I add, "Gotcha! Melissa was supposed to stay at latchkey today."

The rest of the drive home is unusually quiet.

THE ALTERNATE

An alternate bus driver is on standby to fill in on any route not being covered due to vacation or illness. It is sometimes a challenge to drive a route you are not familiar with since you don't know the stops or recognize the children.

One dark rainy morning, the dispatcher hands an alternate driver a piece of paper with special instructions. Before the driver starts his route on the west side of the city, he is to go to an address on the east side and pick up three Ukrainian elementary children who do not speak any English. The children are to be dropped off at a building at the end of the route on the west side of the city.

The directions lead the driver into a subdivision. He tries to find an address to match the one he was given, but the mailboxes are on the opposite side of the road and he can't easily see the numbers. Being able to make out a few numbers, he knows he is getting close.

Suddenly four children appear at the end of a driveway. He activates the overhead lights and opens the door. He gives the children a big smile and they all grin in return as they silently sit down.

The trip to the west side of the city is about fifteen miles and takes a good twenty minutes. Finally, the driver turns off the main road into a subdivision to start the regular stops. It is at this point when one of the students gently taps the driver on the shoulder and says, in *perfect* English, "Bus driver, where are we going?"

The driver quickly stops the bus, turns around in his seat, and says, "You're not from the Ukraine?"

"Where is *that*?" the girl replies.

At this moment, the dispatcher's voice comes over the radio: "Have you picked up the Ukrainian children yet?"

"No, I have not. Although I have managed to kidnap four children from the east side."

A TRACK STAR IS BORN

It is morning. I pull into a subdivision with a road that encircles it. There is a bus stop at the beginning and end of this road. After the students board at the first stop, I check for runners (late students), see none, close the door, and head for the next stop. "Here comes Johnny!" shouts one of the passengers.

I look into the rearview mirror and see Johnny jumping off his porch a few doors back and running around the house to cut through the subdivision toward the next bus stop. As we proceed around the subdivision, I can see him sprinting across yards, jumping fences and hedges, and dodging lawn furniture and swing sets trying to beat me to the end of the circular road.

I give in to the devilish urge to speed up a little. Each time I go faster, his pace increases. The students on the bus are cheering him on.

We arrive at the last stop and I open the door. It is only a few seconds before Johnny leaps onto the bus and the students give him a standing ovation.

A new track star is born!

THREE-SECOND WARNING

Fast reflexes are mandatory for school bus drivers, especially when they are transporting young children.

It is the morning run and I have a load of elementary students. On the route to school is a steep winding descent with a T-intersection at the bottom of a hill. Across the intersection is a large bay.

I have both hands firmly gripping the steering wheel, the bus is geared down, and the air brakes are hissing as I prepare to stop fifteen tons of bus—when a small hand taps me on the shoulder. The young lad says, "I'm sick," which means that in *three seconds* he is going to hurl!

Quickly releasing my right hand, I snatch the wastebasket and hold it in front of the boy. Eighty percent hits the basket. As I bring the bus to a halt at the intersection, I reach over and pull the yellow brake knob, and grab a box of Handiwipes as he finishes depositing his breakfast.

Luckily his parents fed him cereal. And we didn't go into the bay.

"WHAT are you doing?"

WHACK! WHACK!

In the early morning darkness, freezing rain is transforming the bus into a large frozen pumpkin. As I pick up some students at a residential street stop, I realize the foldout stop sign with the flashing lights is not extended as it should be. The next stop is on a busy two-way street where students have to cross. The sign must be operational for this stop.

I get up from the driver's seat, reach underneath it, and pull out the tire checker club. Grasping the club, which resembles a police officer's nightstick, I turn to the bus full of students and say, "I'll be right back."

I exit the bus and walk around the front to the driver's side. I find what I expected: ice has encased the stop sign to the side of the bus. I take the club and forcefully hit the side of the bus several times, until the ice falls off and the sign is able to unfold.

As I climb back on the bus, with the club still in my hand, I glance at the students. Their eyes and mouths are open wide as they watch my every move. From the middle of the bus a small nervous voice says, "*What* are you doing?"

I realize that inside the big metal container, each whack must have sounded like a loud gong.

Everyone was wide awake for the remainder of the ride.

LOST VOICE

One of the pitfalls of being a bus driver for fifty elementary kids is the constant exposure to many viruses. I had finally succumbed to someone's germs, resulting in laryngitis.

While I was driving, I noticed in the mirror several students were out of their seats and standing up. I grabbed the mike to tell them to sit down—but could only muster a hoarse whisper—which could not be heard over the noise in the bus. Not to be outwitted, I extended the mike towards the ceiling speaker and pressed the button. The immediate feedback of *EEEEEEEEEEE* resulted. I now saw a busload of kids with their mouths wide open—but not a sound coming out.

I whispered, "Please, remain seated until we arrive at school."

They all quietly sat down.

On the rest of the trip to school, whenever I noticed a student starting to stand up, I held the mike up in the air and they immediately sat down. It was one of the quietest trips we ever had.

A CLOTHING DISASTER

I regularly drive a small group of special needs children to the public swimming pool. As a part of this task, I assist the male aide in helping the boys change into their swimsuits, get into the pool, shower, etc.

One morning, the aide was absent so the teacher asked me if I could handle the boys by myself. "No problem," I said. How hard could it be to help three visually impaired boys in the men's shower room?

After an hour of swimming, we returned to the men's room to shower. Things were going well—until it was time to put on their street clothes. I soon realized I had mixed up their clothes. The three boys were about the same size and build, so I had no clue as to who was wearing what.

Oh, well. I did the best I could . . . which must not have been very good as the teacher got a puzzled look on her face as soon as she saw the boys. I had to confess the mix-up and that I had no idea who was dressed in whose clothes.

FLAG STOP

Each and every school bus stop is selected and approved based on the safety of the children, visibility of other motorists, etc. "Courtesy stops" by the driver are strictly forbidden and considered a serious safety violation.

On my morning route, I first stop at the top of a subdivision and then continue down the hill to the back of the sub. One day, as I am returning up the hill and rounding a curve, in the headlights of the bus I see a woman wearing a pink bathrobe and fuzzy slippers standing in the middle of the road, waving her arms in the air.

To avoid hitting her, I stop the bus and wait for her to move aside. I then watch as she motions to her son to cross the road and get on the bus. He obviously had missed the bus so she decided to create a new flag stop.

When I returned the bus to the garage, I handed an incident report to the dispatcher and said, "*You* call her!

"So, how many years have you been riding the bus?"

HOW MANY YEARS?

The seats on a school bus are especially designed with high padded backs to cushion students in case of a sudden stop or an accident. Because of this feature, children are usually in the third grade or older before they can actually see over the seats in front of them. And kindergarten and first grade children even have a difficult time looking out the windows.

Whenever I drive a bus with small children I continually see heads popping up and down in the mirror. They are aware of the rule that they have to stay seated at all times while the bus is moving, so to avoid being caught, they quickly stand up to look and then immediately sit back down. In the mirror, it is like watching popcorn pop.

On the early morning route, I pick up junior high, senior high, and parochial school children; so I have kindergarten through twelfth grade students riding together every day. We are one big family.

One day, a try-to-be-cool senior high student turns to the kindergartner in the seat behind him and asks, "So, how many years have you been riding the bus?"

FIZZZZZZZ

During the last week of school in early June, elementary school kids are usually treated to a field trip.

I have transported about fifty third graders to a miniature golf course and pizza parlor. It is a warm, sunny afternoon.

When the kids board the bus for the return ride to school, it is hot inside the bus. Just before I close the door, one of the teachers hands me an unopened liter bottle of orange soda. I put it underneath the dash next to the firewall of the bus so that it is out of the way.

As we proceed back to school, one of the children asks me to turn on the air conditioning. I grab the mike and announce, "This bus is equipped with a sophisticated AC system called twenty-forty. You put all twenty windows down and I will get this bus going forty miles an hour!"

Near school, the bus must climb a long steep hill. The engine is laboring under the full load of students and the temperature gauge is rising. Suddenly I hear *POP!* followed by *FIZZZZZZZZ.* I look down in time to see the bottle of orange soda madly spinning underneath the dash. A second later, the bottle shoots down the aisle like a rocket, spraying orange pop everywhere. The children are jumping, laughing, and screaming with delight.

After the sticky children unload, I remember the school has a garden hose. I drive the bus up a small grade, open the front service door and back emergency door, and hose it out.

All clean, except for my orange socks.

FLAP FASTER

The school bus, which is notorious for being slow on *level* ground, comes to a virtual crawl on the steep grade of the hill I encounter while transporting a bus load of students on a field trip.

I grab the mike and announce, "Everybody put your arms straight up! Now, put your arms out in front of you! Flap them up and down so we can lighten the load on the bus!" Looking in the student mirror, I see the kids flapping their arms. The speedometer drops below twenty-five miles per hour, the gas pedal is to the floor, and the engine labors as we near the crest of the hill. I say, "Keep flapping. We are almost there. We made it!"

As we reach the top of the hill, one of the students notices a giant wind turbine that produces electricity for the city below. He asks about the windmill. I quickly respond, "That is a big fan they turn on to blow cool northern air down into town on hot days."

The teacher, who is sitting behind me, immediately interjects, "Our bus driver, Mr. Bill, is a little windy himself!" She then explains to the students how a wind turbine actually makes electricity.

Seventh through Twelfth Grade

ADOLESCENCE TO RELATIONSHIPS

APRIL FOOLS'

It is Wednesday, March 29. I am driving a busload of sleepy junior high students to school in the dark hours just before dawn. Without warning, I loudly announce over the bus PA, "Listen up, everyone. The school administration is concerned about jokes and pranks on April Fools'. So, there will be no school on April first this year."

The bus erupts in cheers. Eventually the students settle down with jubilant smiles on their faces. Never have I seen such happiness so early in the morning.

Then, a few minutes later, an astute student shouts, "Hey! April first is on Saturday!!"

To which I reply, "April Fools'!"

THANKS FOR THE TIP

It is a particularly cold winter morning and the pro-heater on the bus keeps tripping out, which means there is no heat and the interior of the bus is frigid. Several times along the route, I stop the bus, get out, and reset the heater—only to have it quit working again.

The students are unusually quiet this morning. Maybe they are concentrating on staying warm, since they wear little warm clothing—never hats, gloves, or heavy coats.

As the students get off the bus at school, one of the departing young ladies accuses me of turning off the heat because they were disruptive. "And," she adds, "if you leave the heat on next time, we will be quiet."

I thank her and say, "That is a great idea!" I had never considered using heat as a behavior modification tool.

MORNING SHOWER

Spring has finally arrived. The sun is visible on this morning drive. Lawns are green. Flowers bloom. Birds chirp along the route. I enter a subdivision and see a group of junior high girls and boys waiting in the yard on the corner. I can tell the girls spent an hour primping and getting dressed. Most of the boys look like they just tumbled out of bed.

I stop the bus, with overhead lights flashing. Suddenly, a sprinkler head pops up directly in front of the open door and begins to spray copious amounts of water in every direction.

A melee breaks out among the screaming girls. Books and hair are flying. The girls bump and stumble into one another as they try to avoid the water. Some have slipped on the wet grass and mud.

I quickly close the bus door to prevent more water from coming inside. I release the air brake and pull forward about thirty feet, reset the brake, and open the door. The girls are drenched. The mascara and makeup they meticulously applied runs down their faces and their hair is hanging like an Irish setter's that has just been given a bath.

As they board the bus, I pass out paper towels.

The boys—as you guessed—are laughing and dry as can be.

TOTALLY LOST

As an alternate driver, I am in an unfamiliar subdivision on a dark morning. The road winds around hills and woods and the only visible street signs are small brown ones on stakes. I am getting frustrated trying to find a particular address.

My passengers are special needs adults with multiple handicaps. They try to help me— but each one is giving me different directions—at the same time. The situation finally turns humorous when *everyone* agrees on something: *I am totally lost!*

At that moment, the dispatcher calls me on the radio. A parent has phoned the bus garage to tell him I have driven past her house three times. Apparently I am driving in circles!

I am told to make another pass and she will flag me down.

THE OLDIES

My first run of the morning is a junior high route before sunrise, i.e., it is pitch-black outside. One day, as the kids are unloading at school, a female student hesitates at the door and asks me why I always play the oldies radio station. "Because it works," I reply.

With a puzzled look, she asks, "What do you mean?"

"We have over fifty students on this bus. When I play the oldies station, they sleep!"

"No shoes, no service!"

SHOES REQUIRED

I slow the bus and turn on the overhead lights for a designated morning stop. I do not see the young man who is usually at this stop, so I honk the horn. A second later, he jumps off his porch and runs full tilt across the yard toward the bus—when both of his shoes fly off his feet! (Obviously he had not tied them.)

When he arrives at the bus door with bare feet, I say, "Sorry, shoes required."

A second later, after the laughter on the bus subsides, I tell him to go back for his shoes and that we will wait for him.

"Welcome aboard. Are you a new student?"

STEAMY WINDOWS

One junior high coed on my morning route was always dressed in black. I mean, *everything* was black. Her hair. Her fingernails. Her lipstick. Even her jewelry. And, whenever I opened the door for her to board the bus, the windows would completely steam over. Which didn't make any sense because my daily greeting of "Good morning!" was always met with an *icy* stare.

It soon became a habit for me to activate the defrosters full blast before I arrived at her stop—but to no avail. I would *always* have to wipe the inside of the windshield with a cloth in order to proceed after she came on the bus. This continued through four long months of winter.

One day, an unfamiliar student with blonde hair and dressed in pink was waiting by herself at the stop. As the girl climbed onto the bus, I said, "Good morning! Are you a new student?"

She gave me a big smile and said, "Don't you recognize me? I ride every day!"

As I contemplated her new look and grabbed the cloth to wipe the windshield, I realized the windows were clear. They were not steamed over.

I know there must be a logical reason for this, like melting snow that was tracked in by the kids before her, causing humidity in the bus that automatically reacted to the cold air when I opened the door for her—but I never had the windshield steam up again. Strange!

NO BUS PASS

The morning fog is thick and visibility is low. I am trying to find a mailbox with a particular number on it. I see movement in the driveway up ahead. I quickly hit the switch for the overhead lights, slow to a stop, and open the door.

Instead of a sleepy student, a doe with a startled look on its face greets me.

As the students burst out laughing, I quickly say to the deer, "No pass. No ride," and close the door.

Later, I add this incident to my list of false student sightings, such as mailboxes, garbage cans, bushes, joggers, and a guy in his bathrobe going out to get his morning paper.

"You're LATE! Look what you've done!"

MY FAULT

It is extremely cold and windy this morning, and I am running late on the junior high route. At a regular stop I open the door and a young lady with long hair sticking out every which way climbs on board. Before taking a seat, she pauses by the door and says in an angry voice, "You're late. Look what you have done!"

Her hair is frozen. She looks like the Greek goddess Medusa.

I try to keep my composure, but when the other kids explode into laughter . . . so do I.

FOUR EYES

After unloading students at the junior high school, I always drive the bus forward to the parking lot and check it for lost objects, sleeping students, etc. before returning to the bus garage.

This particular morning, I find a pair of eyeglasses lying on a seat. They might be important to one of the students, so I decide to take them into the office.

As I am walking to the school entrance, I notice a girl who rides my bus standing still and squinting towards the parking lot. "Try these on," I suggest. "You might see better."

She takes the glasses and puts them on. "Thank you," she says. "But, how did you know they were mine?"

"It was easy," I reply.

BE CAREFUL OF WHAT YOU AGREE TO

A fellow bus driver returns a busload of students to school. They have been on a morning field trip. Since it is lunchtime, the driver decides to dine in the school cafeteria.

As he eats his lunch, several students that normally ride his daily route join him. After they have taken a few bites of food, one of the students says, "This stuff really stinks."

The driver unconsciously agrees with a mumbled, "Uh-huh."

Immediately, one of the boys yells in a voice that would rival the school PA system, "COOKIE, THE BUS DRIVER SAYS YOUR FOOD REALLY STINKS!"

The driver's eyes open wide when he hears the sound of the kitchen door burst open. He sees the head cook, with a red face and a look that could kill, wiping her hands on her apron as she heads towards him.

Later, as he sits in the principal's office writing a letter of apology to the cook, he thinks, "This is not what I had in mind for my lunch break."

ALIENS ON THE BUS

All of the senior high students seem to be carrying rubber gloves. I inquire and am informed they are studying first aid. As we make our stops, the expected blowing up of the gloves ensues.

Looking in the mirror, I observe one boy pull a glove over his head and nose. He is breathing in through his mouth and exhaling via his nose, which makes the fingers of the glove fill with air and expand. The others quickly follow suit, until the bus is full of aliens.

We received many startled looks from passing motorists that day!

BEWARE OF EMPTY PARKING LOTS

As I was driving a girl's track team to a meet, the coach requested we stop for a bite to eat. Not knowing the area, I spotted a Burger King. After unloading the girls, I drove around the corner to look for a place to park the bus. There wasn't any available space, but then I noticed an empty parking lot next door. I parked the bus next to the building behind a large sign and walked across the back of the lot to the fast-food joint.

After everyone was finished eating, we left the restaurant together and they followed me back to the bus. I was standing by the door of the bus as the girls boarded when I noticed cars slowing down and people gawking in our direction. Looking around, I realized the building was painted PURPLE!

As we drove out of the parking lot, my worst fears were confirmed. In large letters the sign said: **Velvet Touch Gentleman's Club. New girls starring nightly**.

BLUE KID

While driving the bus on the afternoon route home, we are traveling over a road with tremendous potholes, a.k.a., tank traps. I hit one hard and look in the mirror to make sure everyone is still seated. They are.

However, a couple of seconds later I hear, "I need some paper towel." I look in the mirror again and see a blue face staring in my direction. Apparently he had been taking a drink of Gatorade when we hit the pothole.

"I think you just discovered the reason for the rule of no food or drink on the bus," I say as I hand him the paper towel.

KEEP YOUR HAIR TO YOURSELF

It is spring. The afternoon is warm and the senior high school students are frisky—especially the boys. I notice a group of them unbuttoning their shirts and showing off their chest hairs (or lack thereof) to the girls. A contest starts and one young man is declared the winner.

But, his conquest is quickly deflated when he stands up to show off his chest and a precocious young lady reaches over and yanks a handful of hair, resulting in his primal scream of pain.

RITE OF PASSAGE

When most kids reach the age of sixteen or seventeen they start driving to school instead of riding the bus. One boy, who was a particularly active teenager, i.e., I continually gave him warnings to stay seated, announced that this was his last bus ride because he was getting his driver's license the following day. My response was, "I give you two weeks before you're back on the bus."

Three days later, while I was supervising the boarding ramp at school, he walked by with three other boys who usually rode my bus. They were excitedly talking about his car.

My route from school has a series of curves and then a straightaway. As we rounded a curve, I saw a police car with its overhead lights on and a vehicle pulled over to the side. Four teenage boys were standing beside the stopped car.

I was wrong.

It was only three days before he was back on my bus.

A LIKELY STORY

In the afternoon, as the senior high students board the bus for a ride home, I supervise the ramp and incoming busses; therefore, I do not see all of the students—or what they are carrying—as they actually get on my bus.

I have stopped the bus to drop off a student in her neighborhood when, all of a sudden, several empty beer bottles clatter down the aisle toward me. Exiting the driver's seat to investigate, I find a young lady with beer bottles taped together in the seat beside her. She quickly explains that she participated in a science contest to build a tower that would hold a bowling ball—and she won.

As I hand her the empty glass containers, I realize we are getting strange looks from the drivers in the cars that are patiently waiting.

When I imagine the phone calls the dispatcher will most surely receive, I calmly suggest to her that soda bottles would have been a better choice.

THE GRAND SLIDE

At the beginning of each school year, I introduce myself to the students as Mr. Bill. Then I repeat my name and tell them that if they have something nice to say to the administration about my driving to remember my name is Mr. Bill. But, if they have any complaints about my driving, my name is Steve.

One extremely icy afternoon, as I am driving a busload of junior high students home, we encounter a steep hill that looks as if the Zamboni from the local hockey rink had just passed over it. We are about halfway down the hill as I approach a student's house. The overhead lights are flashing and I lightly apply the air brakes. Suddenly the back of the bus starts to slide. This is *not* what a bus driver wants with a busload of kids.

Every maneuver I make, turning into the skid, pumping the air brakes, etc. is to no avail. The bus makes a ninety degree turn to the left and comes to an abrupt halt in the student's driveway. I quickly lock the air brakes, open the door, turn to the students, and say, "Welcome to our new front-door service!"

In spite of my attempt to lighten the situation, the students are silent—until a male voice from the back of the bus yells, "Hey, Steve, let's see you do it again!"

EPILOGUE

During summer break, many bus drivers volunteer their time to work the admissions booth at the county fair. The proceeds for the hours we work are donated to the school scholarship and humanitarian fund. The fair is held in the middle of August.

I am in the booth, which has a window screen with a small opening to take money and hand out tickets. The sun is bright and the glare makes it hard for the fair goers to see me. The admission price is $3.00 for adults and $1.00 for twelve-year-olds and under.

Two girls approach my window. The first girl asks for one adult ticket. The second girl says, "I am twelve."

"Let me see," I reply. "You go to East Junior High, you will be in the eighth grade, you live on Blossom Road, ride bus 303, and your driver is Mr. Bill."

"HOW DO YOU KNOW ALL THIS?!" she exclaims.

"I am Mr. Bill. That will be three dollars, please."

You never know where your bus driver will be.

ABOUT THE AUTHOR

BILL PARRISH

After thirty years in retail management and eleven years in business consulting—positions that required moving our family too many times to count—retiring in quiet Northern Michigan was a welcome change. My wife and I looked forward to settling down and enjoying our children and grandchildren.

The best part for me, though, was not having to set the alarm clock to wake up early in the morning. I could relax. Spend my days as I wished.

As part of our new carefree lifestyle, my wife and I decided to participate in a senior swim class at the local civic center. We soon realized that after the seniors swam, a group of special needs children used the pool. We have a special needs grandson and when a request was made for adults with experience handling special needs children in the pool, we volunteered. This led to an offer for my wife to work as a teacher's assistant in their classroom.

Now, with her getting up early each weekday morning came the question: What are you going to do besides sleep in every day?

"Hmmm, I replied, "maybe I will drive the school bus."

I inquired, was hired, and attended bus driving school. This part-time job only lasted one week before they offered me a full-time position with great benefits. I went home to discuss the offer with my wife.

"I will set the five a.m. alarm for you," was her answer.

Spending time with children of all ages provides many opportunities for humor. After talking about funny incidents with my wife and friends, it was suggested that I write them down. I did. And thus, this book.

So, after forty years of working with type A personalities I drive a large yellow bus at five miles per hour under the speed limit, with frequent stops—which frustrates the heck out of the type A's rushing to work. I do pull over to the side of the road to let them pass when it is safely possible, but a word of caution: NEVER honk your horn at a school bus. Revenge is sweet! It is easily within my power to make type A's follow the bus all the way into town and wait at every stop and railroad along the way!

You may e-mail Bill Parrish at:

yellowbuspublish@aol.com

ABOUT THE ILLUSTRATOR

Dick Evans—illustrator, cartoonist, and drawing instructor—was born with a pen in his hand—or so it seems. Ever since he was a teenager, he has combined his drawing talent and quick wit to create humorous cartoons and illustrations.

In 1977, he decided to share his love of cartoons by becoming a part-time drawing instructor. In addition to teaching classes to students of all ages, including adults, through Northwestern Michigan College in Traverse City, Michigan, he also travels to grade schools and other locations. "Have pen, will travel" is his motto.

Best known as the instructor of Cartoon FUNdamentals, Dick Evans focuses on individual creativity and stresses only one classroom rule: You can't do it wrong. He believes everyone has an artist lurking inside him or her that is only waiting to be released.

His work has appeared in numerous local, state, and national publications, including a cartoon strip titled "Bear Pause," which was featured in *Catch, The Entertainment News* published by *Traverse, The Magazine.*

Dick Evans is the creator of Tourist Country Bear, a.k.a. TC Bear, who is featured in *Up North with TC Bear*, a coloring book that highlights tourist activities in Northern Michigan.

When asked if he ever did character sketches of coworkers or clients, Dick Evans replied, "Why, I would never do that . . . at least not while they were looking!"

To contact Dick Evans and to see more of his work, please visit:

www.bearclausepublications.com

ORDER INFORMATION

To order additional copies of the *Adventures of Mr. Bill* and to inquire about quantity discounts, please visit:

www.yellowbuspublishing.com